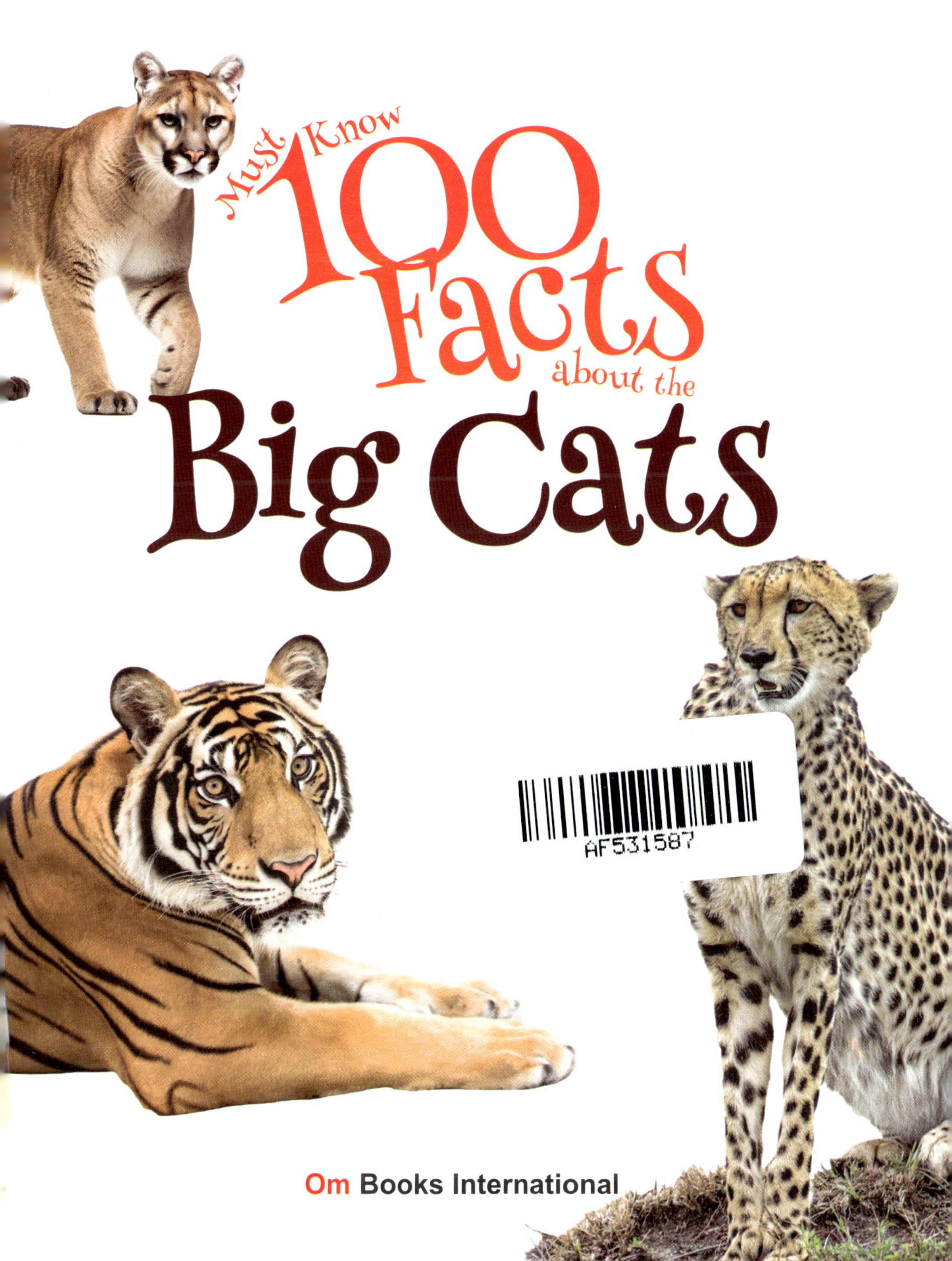

Must Know 100 Facts about the Big Cats

Om Books International

First Published in 2025 by

Om Books International

Corporate & Editorial Office
A-12, Sector 64, Noida 201 301
Uttar Pradesh, India
Phone: +91 120 477 4100
Email: editorial@ombooks.com
Website: www.ombooksinternational.com

Sales Office
107, Ansari Road, Darya Ganj
New Delhi 110 002, India
Phone: +91 11 4000 9000
Email: sales@ombooks.com
Website: www.ombooks.com

ISBN: 978-93-52761-79-1

Printed in India

10 9 8 7 6 5 4 3 2 1

CONTENTS

Prowess of the Predators 4–5

Habitat and Home 6–7

Diet and Hunting Techniques 8–9

Conservation Efforts and Threats 10–11

Unique Adaptations and Behaviours 12–13

The Language of Roars and Growls 14–15

Cubs and Reproduction 16–17

Iconic Markings and Camouflage 18–19

The Role of Big Cats in Ecosystems 20–21

Interactions with Humans 22–23

Survival Skills and Instincts 24–25

Reproductive Behaviours and Family Dynamics 26–27

Big Cats Across the Globe 28–29

Cub Class: The Early lives of Big Cats 30–31

Big Cats in Culture and Mythology 32–33

Conservation Heroes and Initiatives 34–35

Big Cats and Human Impact 36–37

Jaws and Claws: The Anatomy of Predation 38–39

The Puma: America's Athletic Cat 40–41

Echoes of the Past: Extinct Big Cats 42–43

Beauty that Puts Lives at Risk 44–45

Furry Relatives of the Big Cats 46–47

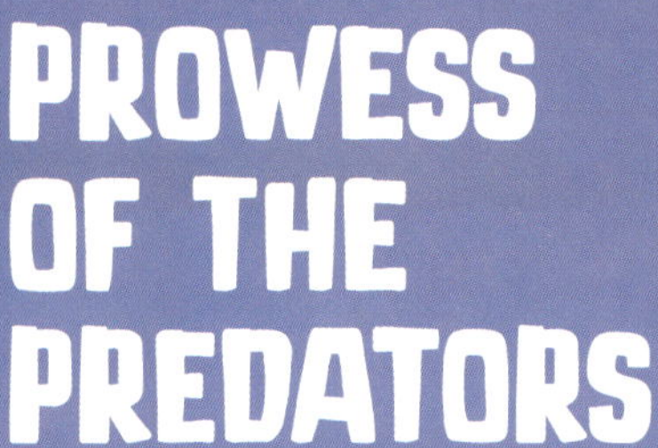

THE SPEED SPRINTER: CHEETAH'S INCREDIBLE SPEED

The cheetah is the fastest animal on land. It can run as fast as 112 km/h (70 mph). It can cover large distances in a short time. It uses its strong legs and super flexible spine to run really fast.

Fun Fact

Tigers have striped skin, not just striped fur. The unique pattern helps them blend in and hide in the wild.

NIGHT VISION NAVIGATORS: THE LEOPARD'S LUMINOUS EYES

Leopards have a highly developed sense of night vision, allowing them to see almost six times better in the dark than humans. They have special eyes with lots of rod cells and a reflective layer behind the retina that help them see in the dark. This helps them hunt under the cover of night.

ROARING RULERS: THE LION'S MIGHTY ROAR

A lion's roar can be heard from as far as 8 kilometres (5 miles) away. Lions roar to tell other animals to stay away and to talk to distant members of their pride. Their speciallarynx and vocal cords help them make such a loud roar.

STEALTHY STALKERS: JAGUAR'S JAW STRENGTH

Jaguars have the strongest bite of any big cat compared to their size. Their powerful jaws and muscular build can crush hard things, like skulls and shells of their prey. They are great hunters on land and in water.

SOLITARY BUT STRONG: THE TIGER'S MIGHTY SPACE

Tigers need lots of space, sometimes up to 100 square kilometres to live. They mark their area with scents, growls and their presence to tell other tigers to stay away and avoid fights.

HABITAT AND HOME

Fun Fact

Leopards live in more types of habitats than any other big cat, including forests, mountains, grasslands, and deserts across Africa and Asia.

MOUNTAIN MONARCHS: SNOW LEOPARDS OF THE PEAKS

Snow leopards live in the high mountain ranges of Central Asia, sometimes as high as 18,000 feet. Their thick fur and fur-covered feet act as natural snowshoes in the harsh, cold environments.

JUNGLE JUGGERNAUTS: THE AMAZONIAN JAGUAR

Jaguars are the largest big cats in the Americas. They are mainly found in the dense rainforests of the Amazon Basin. They are skilled swimmers and often live inareas close to water bodies such as rivers and lakes.

DESERT DWELLERS: THE LEOPARD'S DESERT SURVIVAL

The Arabian leopard lives in dry, semi-desert areas where water is difficult to find. Their survival in such environments shows their amazing adaptability among big cats.

GRASSLAND GUARDIANS: CHEETAHS

Cheetahs have a light tan or golden undercoat with solid black spots. Unlike leopards and jaguars, their spots are solid, not open, making this a useful identifying characteristic.

FOREST FORTRESSES

The endangered Sumatran tiger lives in the thick tropical forests of Sumatra, Indonesia. These forests provide crucial cover and a rich supply of prey.

DIET AND HUNTING TECHNIQUES

Fun Fact

A tiger's whiskers are so sensitive that they can feel their prey move, even in complete darkness. This helps them hunt at night.

PRECISION POUNCERS

Lions are one of the few big cats that hunt in groups. They use complex team tactics like circling around prey before charging, to trap and take down prey. This teamwork shows how skilled they are as top predators.

SLEALTHY HUNTERS

Tigers hunt alone, using stealth and power to catch their prey. They use their body stripes as hiding in the dense forest, stalking close enough to launch a powerful attack.

OPPORTUNISTIC OMNIVORES

Unlike many other big cats that focus on large herbivores, jaguars have a diverse diet. They eat over 85 different species of animals, ranging from fish and reptiles to birds and mammals.

SELECTIVE SPRINTERS

Cheetahs hunt by vision rather than scent, selecting weak or young animals from a herd. They then start a fast chase that lasts 20 to 30 seconds. They only catch their prey about half the time, so every run is a big risk.

HIGH ALTITUDE HUNTERS

Snow leopards are master hunters in the mountains. Their fur helps them blend in, so they can sneak up on animals without being seen. Then, they jump down from above to catch their prey.

CONSERVATION EFFORTS AND THREATS

TIGER CONSERVATION CHALLENGES

With all subspecies of wild tigers endangered, conservation efforts focus on preventing habitat loss, poaching, and illegal wildlife trade. Protected areas and wildlife corridors have become vital to the survival of these majestic animals.

Fun Fact

Leopards are capable of dragging prey up to three times their weight up into trees to avoid scavengers.

TRADING FOR SURVIVAL

Leopard skins and body parts are often sold illegally in wildlife trade markets. Efforts to protect them include strict enforcement of wildlife protection laws and international treaties like Convention on International Trade in Endangered Species of Wild Fauna and Flora (CITIES), to stop poaching and illegal trade.

CHEETAH'S SHRINKING GENE POOL

Cheetahs have a small gene pool, meaning they don't have much variety in their genes. This makes them more likely to get sick and harder to adapt to changes. People are working to protect their homes and study their genes to help them stay healthy.

JAGUARS AND WETLAND CONSERVATION

As wetland dwellers, jaguars play a crucial role in maintaining the ecological balance of their habitats. Protecting these areas is not only about saving the big cat but also about preserving the entire ecosystem they support.

SNOW LEOPARD'S RISING RISKS

Snow leopards live in high mountains, but climate change is making their homes harder to live in. It affects the availability of prey and the places they live. People are working to help them by finding ways to protect their habitats from these changes.

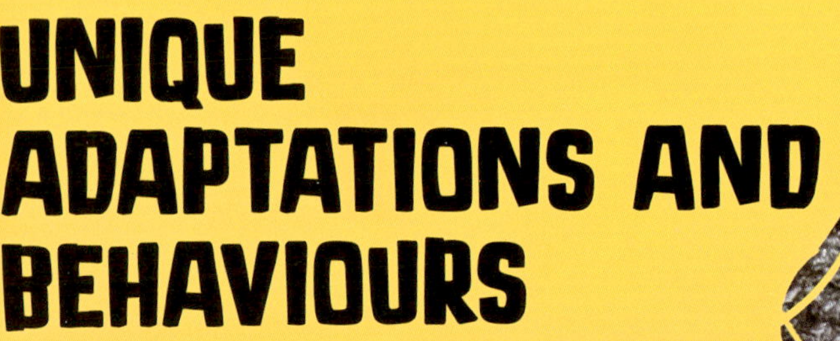

UNIQUE ADAPTATIONS AND BEHAVIOURS

Fun Fact

Jaguars have a unique killing their prey. They bite through the skull, between the ears to deliver a fatal bite to the brain.

WATER-LOVING FELINES

Unlike most cats, tigers are excellent swimmers and often use water bodies to cool down or hunt prey that lives in water. They can be frequently seen relaxing in ponds, lakes, and rivers during the heat of the day.

CHEETAH'S RUDDER-LIKE TAIL

A cheetah's tail plays a critical role during its high-speed chases, acting like a rudder to steer and balance at incredible speeds. It helps it to make sharp turns while chasing fast prey.

LEOPARDS AND TREE CLIMBING

Leopards are among the best climbers of the big cat family. They use trees to stay safe, store food, and get a good view. Their strong legs and flexible bodies help them climb up and down easily.

SNOW LEOPARDS AND THEIR LONESOME LIFESTYLE

Snow leopards are very lonely big cats, often roaming alone over vast areas. They rarely interact with other snow leopards except when mothers are raising their cubs.

JAGUAR LIFESTYLE

Jaguars hunt alone and can travel more than six miles a day to find prey. They mark their home areas.

THE LANGUAGE OF ROARS AND GROWLS

Fun Fact

A lion's roar can reach up to 114 decibels at a distance of about 1 metre.

THE SOCIAL CALLS OF LIONS

Lions use various sounds within their pride, including roars, grunts, and moans. These help in hunting, maintain group cohesion, and warn off strangers. Each lion's roar is unique and can be recognised by others in their pride.

TIGER'S TERRITORIAL WARNING

Tigers growl to warn others to stay away and show their dominance, when protecting their home. Their loud growl can scare off any stranger.

PURRING PREDATORS

Cheetahs are capable of purring, a sound they make when content or to comfort their young. This purring occurs both when inhaling and exhaling, different from domestic cats who only purr while exhaling.

WHISPER IN THE WILDERNESS

Leopards communicate through a series of soft calls, chuffs, and growls. These sounds help mothers stay close to their cubs and help animals live alone in the forest.

THE SILENT STALKER

Snow leopards are among the least vocal of the big cats. They do not roar but communicate through hisses, growls, and mews. Their quiet nature helps them stay hidden inthe mountains, essential for hunting.

CUBS AND REPRODUCTION

Fun Fact

Leopard cubs are born blind and only open their eyes after about 7 days. They are completely dependent on their mother for protection and nourishment during this vulnerable period.

NURSERY NURTURERS

Lionesses in a pride often have cubs at the same time so that all the cubs are about the same age. This allows them to nurse each other's cubs, enhancing survival rates by communal care and protection.

TIGERS' TRAINING SESSIONS

Tiger cubs stay with their mothers for about two years, during which they are taught essential survival skills such as hunting and territory marking. This helps the cubs learn how to be strong predators.

MOUNTAIN MINIATURES

Snow leopard cubs are born in hidden dens lined with their mother's fur for warmth. These cubs are adapted to the cold from birth, growing rapidly to cope with the harsh mountain climate.

CHEETAH CUBS' LEARNING THROUGH PLAY

Cheetah cubs engage in playful activities that help develop their agility and hunting skills. These play sessions are critical for learning the incredible speed and steering they need for chasing prey.

SOLO FROM THE START

Leopard cubs are introduced to solid food at about three months and start learning to hunt by observing their mothers. They become independent earlier than many other big cat species, sometimes as young as eight months.

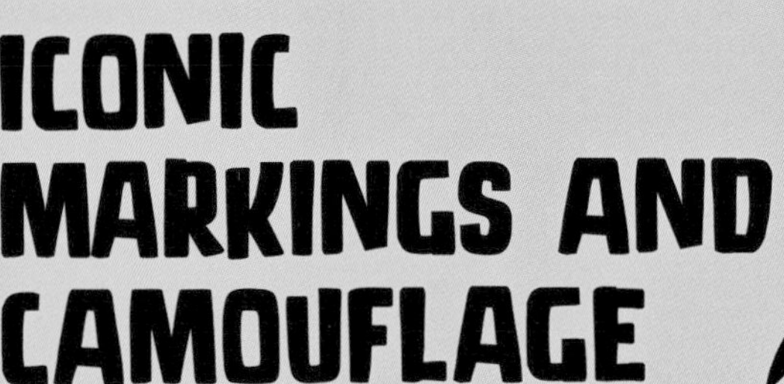

ICONIC MARKINGS AND CAMOUFLAGE

STRIPES FOR STEALTH

Tiger stripes are like human fingerprints; no two tigers have the same pattern. These stripes help them blend into their forest surroundings and making them less visible to prey.

Fun Fact

The pattern on a jaguar's coat is so good at hiding them that they can almost disappear into the jungle with just one step.

LEOPARDS'S SPOTS AND ROSETTES

Leopards have special spots and rosettes on their fur that help them blend into their surroundings. This pattern helps them hide in the wild, making it easier to remain unseen until they strike.

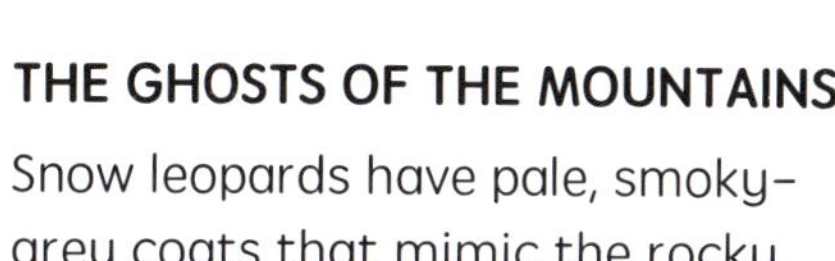

THE GHOSTS OF THE MOUNTAINS

Snow leopards have pale, smoky-grey coats that mimic the rocky mountains. This colouration makes them almost ghostly in appearance, aiding their stealth as they move rocky areas.

CHEETAH'S TEAR MARKS

The black tear marks on a cheetah's face run from the corner of its eyes down the sides of its nose. They help reduce glare from the sun and help in long-distance vision, essential during high-speed chases.

JAGUARS' WATER REFLECTIONS

Jaguars' coats have larger, darker rosettes with thicker lines that help them blend into the shadowy environments of rainforests and wetlands. This pattern works well near water, where it blends with the light shining through.

THE ROLE OF BIG CATS IN ECOSYSTEMS

LIONS AND ECOSYSTEM BALANCE

Lions play a crucial role in maintaining the health of their ecosystems by controlling the population of large plant-eating animals called herbivores. This prevents overgrazing and ensures a diverse and healthy ecosystem.

Fun Fact

Lions can indirectly help control diseases by reducing the number of herbivores, like wildebeests, which can carry ticks that spread illness.

TIGERS AS FOREST GUARDIANS

Tigers help regulate prey populations and maintain the structural integrity of forest ecosystems. By being there, they help protect the variety of plants and animals in the forest.

ENGINEERS OF THE FOREST

Jaguars influence the distribution of plant species in tropical rainforests by predating on a variety of herbivores. As top predators, they keep other animals in balance, which helps protect the whole forest.

MOUNTAIN MONITORS

Snow leopards help regulate prey populations in mountainous areas, which helps maintain plant diversity and ecosystem stability. Their conservation is also crucial for protecting the water sources that originate in their high-altitude habitats.

SPEEDY SEED SPREADERS

Cheetahs contribute to the health of their ecosystems by preying on different herbivores. This helps spread seeds and stops plants from growing too much, which promotes ecological diversity.

INTERACTIONS WITH HUMANS

Fun Fact

Jaguars are often seen as symbols of strength and resilience in many indigenous cultures across the Americas, featuring in myths and legends.

CONFLICTS AND COEXISTENCE

Lions sometimes come into conflict with humans when they prey on livestock. To prevent this, people are building stronger fences for animals and setting up patrols to protect the animals.

THE HUMAN-WILDLIFE INTERFACE

As human populations expand, the overlap between tiger habitats and human settlements increases, leading to conflicts. To help, conservationists are creating safe spaces and pathways to reduce interactions.

JAGUARS AND THE JUNGLE'S EDGE

In areas where forests meet farmland, jaguars may prey on livestock, leading to human–jaguar conflicts. New ideas like paying farmers for lost animals and teaching people how to live with jaguars are being used.

CHEETAHS AND FARMERS

Cheetahs often face threats from farmers who view them as pests due to their occasional attacks on livestock. Conservation programs are using safe methods to protect both cheetahs and farm animals.

HERDERS' CHALLENGES

In the remote mountains, snow leopards are seen as threats by local herders when they attack livestock. The conservationists are offering insurance and building stronger pens to keep both the snow leopards and animals safe.

SURVIVAL SKILLS AND INSTINCTS

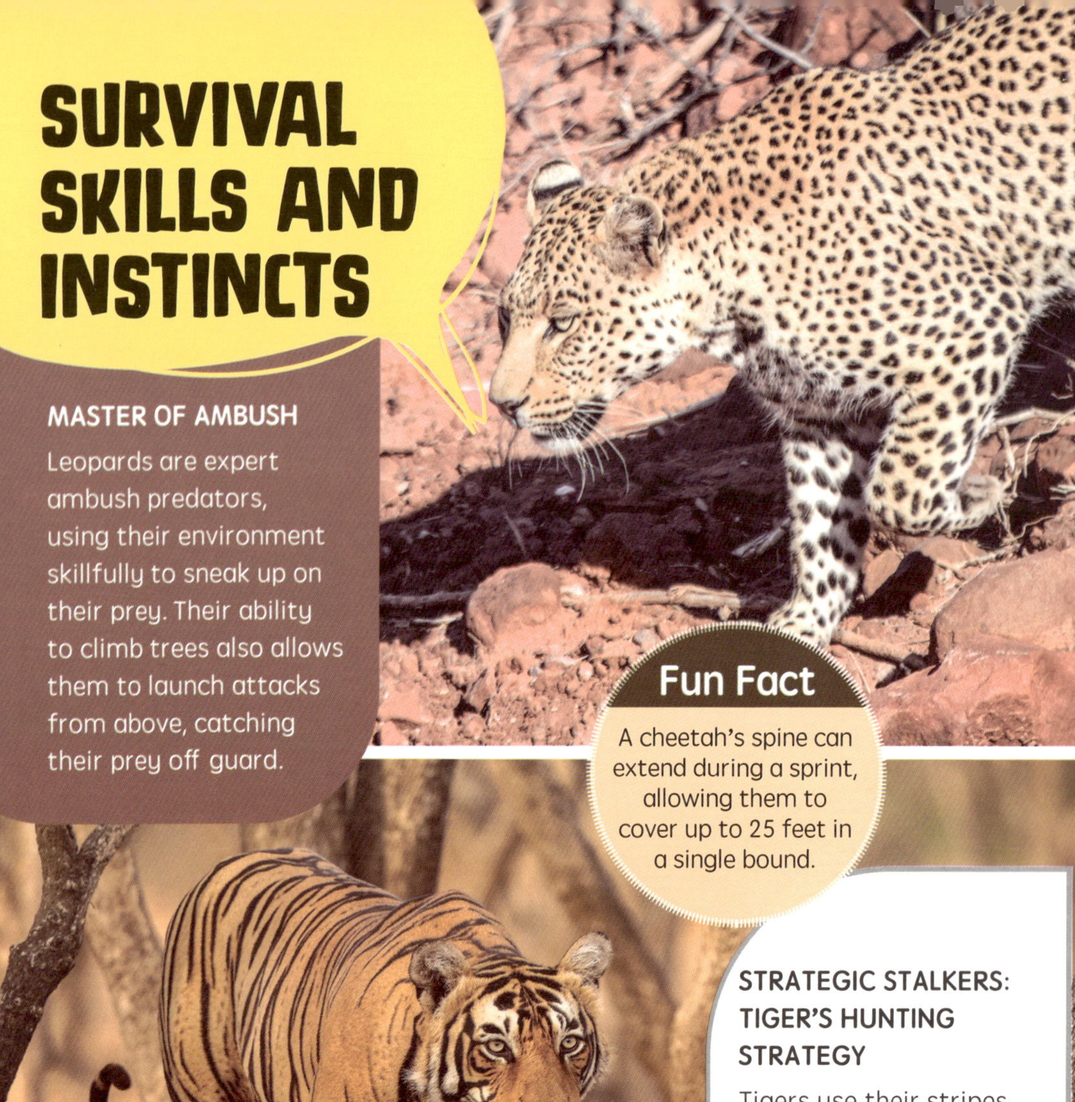

MASTER OF AMBUSH

Leopards are expert ambush predators, using their environment skillfully to sneak up on their prey. Their ability to climb trees also allows them to launch attacks from above, catching their prey off guard.

Fun Fact

A cheetah's spine can extend during a sprint, allowing them to cover up to 25 feet in a single bound.

STRATEGIC STALKERS: TIGER'S HUNTING STRATEGY

Tigers use their stripes to blend into the forest, quietly sneaking up on their prey until they are close enough to attack. Their patience and precision make them one of the most successful solitary predators.

CHEETAH'S CALCULATED CHASE

Cheetahs do not hunt their prey by stealth; they use their speed to catch it. They need open space and perfect timing to make a successful high-speed chase.

JAGUAR'S JAWS

Jaguars have one of the most powerful jaws among big cats. These can crush tough shells, like those of turtles and reptiles. These also helps them eat different kinds of food.

SNOW LEOPARD'S SILENT STEPS

Snow leopards have thickly padded paws that act as natural snow boots, helping them tread silently in their snowy environment. This helps them sneak up on prey in the quiet mountains.

REPRODUCTIVE BEHAVIORS AND FAMILY DYNAMICS

A MOTHER'S COMMITMENT

Female tigers are solitary creatures, fiercely protective of their territory and young. They raise their cubs alone, teaching them to hunt and survive independently until they are ready to claim their own territories.

PRIDE AND PARENTHOOD

Lions are different from other big cats because they live in groups called prides. A pride has adult females, their cubs, and a few adult males. This helps them work together to take care of the cubs and keep them safe.

Fun Fact

Lion cubs are born with blue eyes, which change to brown by the age of two to three months.

NURSERY SECRETS OF LEOPARDS

Leopard mothers are known for their secretive nature when it comes to rearing their young. They move them to different safe places to keep them hidden from predators, including other big cats.

SNOW LEOPARD SOLITUDE

Snow leopards are solitary except when females are raising cubs. Adult snow leopards rarely meet each other, showing how solitary they are.

CHEETAH CUB CARE

Cheetah mothers raise their cubs in isolation, often moving them to new hiding places to protect them from predators. The first few months are crucial, as the death rate among cheetah cubs is high due to predation and competition.

BIG CATS ACROSS THE GLOBE

Fun Fact

All big cats face common threats such as habitat loss, conflict with humans, and poaching.

BIG CAT'S GLOBAL TERRITORIES

Big cats live in different places around the world, like Africa, Europe, Asia, and the Americas. Each big cat is adapted to survive in different environment; from the rainforests and savannas to mountain ranges and cold forests.

THE AMERICAN BIG CATS

In the Americas, jaguars and pumas are top predators. Jaguars live in the thick rainforests of Central and South America, using their strength and swimming skills. Pumas live in many different places, from Canada to the southern Andes, showing how well they can adapt to different environments.

ASIA'S DOMINANT PREDATORS

Tigers, historically found from Turkey to the eastern coasts of Russia, symbolise the wild majesty of Asian forests. These powerful animals occupy diverse habitats, including tropical and evergreen forests, grasslands, and mangrove swamps, each environment hosting different tiger subspecies adapted to local conditions.

AFRICA'S BIG CAT DIVERSITY

Africa is home for big cat diversity, hosting lions, leopards, and cheetahs. Lions are found mostly in the African savannas, but they also live in forests and brush areas. Leopards live in many places, from dry deserts to green forests. Cheetahs prefer open areas in Eastern and Southern Africa, where their speed helps them hunt.

MASTERS OF ADAPTATION

Leopards are the most adaptable big cats. They can live near cities and have been known to survive in places changed by humans. This shows how well they can adjust to different environments.

CUB CLASS: THE EARLY LIVES OF BIG CATS

VULNERABLE BEGINNINGS

Big cat cubs, like those of lions, leopards, and tigers, are born in a vulnerable state, helpless and blind. This initial helplessness makes their first few weeks critical, as they depend entirely on their mother for protection and nourishment. The blindness fades as their eyes open within a week or two after birth.

PATERNAL PARTICIPATION

Contrary to popular belief, male lions sometimes play an important role in the upbringing of cubs. They protect the pride's territory from strangers, ensuring a safe environment for their offspring. This protection helps to prevent rival males from taking over the pride and killing the cubs.

Fun Fact

Lion cubs start to grow their manes at about one year old. By the time they are three to four years old, their manes are fully grown, showing that they have become adults.

LEARNING TO HUNT

Young cubs learn important survival skills, and hunting is one of the most important. They learn by watching their mothers and mimicking their actions. This learning process is essential for developing the techniques they will use to hunt independently in the future. Their mothers show them different tricks, like how to move quietly and when to jump at the right moment.

WHAT'S IN A NAME?

Not all big cat babies are called cubs. For instance, pumas, also known as mountain lions or cougars, refer to their young as kittens. These kittens share many similarities with domestic cat kittens, being playful at first and then learning survival skills before becoming more serious like adults.

THE STRUGGLE FOR SURVIVAL

The journey to adulthood is filled with challenges for big cat cubs. Despite their parents' best efforts to protect and nurture them, many cubs do not survive to adulthood. Threats include predation, starvation, accidents, and disease. In some species, only a small percentage of born cubs make it to adulthood.

BIG CATS IN CULTURE AND MYTHOLOGY

TIGERS: SPIRITUAL AND MYTHICAL CREATURES

In many Asian cultures, tigers are seen as guardians of good fortune and have a significant presence in folklore and spiritual beliefs. They are often depicted as protectors against evil spirits and bad luck.

Fun Fact

In ancient Egypt, lions were connected to the war goddess Sekhmet. She was shown as a lioness and was thought to be a strong protector of the pharaohs and a leader in battles.

LIONS: SYMBOLS OF ROYALTY AND COURAGE

Lions have been revered throughout history in various cultures, symbolising strength, bravery, and royalty. They appear in numerous national emblems and have been featured in folklore and mythology around the world.

JAGUARS: SACRED BEASTS OF THE AMERICAS

Jaguars hold a special place in Native American and Mesoamerican cultures, where they are often associated with the power of the night and the mysteries of the jungle. In some traditions, jaguars are even seen as gods, representing strength and life.

LEOPARDS: ICONS OF STEALTH AND SOLITUDE

Leopards are often depicted in African and Asian mythologies as symbols of cunning and solitary power. Their secretive nature has inspired numerous tales and has made them figures of respect in various tribal cultures.

SNOW LEOPARDS: GHOSTS OF THE MOUNTAINS IN FOLKLORE

Snow leopards are often called the 'ghosts of the mountain' because of their secretive nature. In local stories, people believe they are magical mountain spirits that represent the beauty and mystery of nature.

CONSERVATION HEROES AND INITIATIVES

THE GLOBAL TIGER INITIATIVE

This international effort aims to unite conservationists, governments, and scientists in the battle to double the wild tiger population by 2022. It focuses on habitat preservation and anti-poaching measures.

SAVE THEM!

INTERNATIONAL TIGER DA

Fun Fact

The Asiatic Lion Conservation Project has successfully increased the population of Asiatic lions in India's Gir Forest. It shows thateffective conservation practices can result in recovery for even the most endangered species.

PROJECT SNOW LEOPARD

It was launchedin high-altitude regions across Asia. This project aims to protect the endangered snow leopard and its habitat through community-based conservation efforts and scientific research.

JAGUAR CORRIDOR INITIATIVE

This initiative seeks to connect jaguar populations from Mexico to Argentina through a network of wildlife corridors. This helps in gene flow and increases the chances of survival for this American big cat.

CHEETAH OUTREACH: AN AMBASSADOR FOR WILD CHEETAHS

Founded in South Africa, this program educates communities on the importance of cheetah conservation. It includes ambassador cheetahs that help raise awareness and support for cheetah conservation projects.

AFRICAN LEOPARD GPS COLLARING PROJECT

Conservationists use GPS to track leopard's movements and behaviour. This helps them learn where leopard's live and how they interact with people, so they can find better ways to prevent problems between them.

BIG CATS AND HUMAN IMPACT

Fun Fact

In some cultures, wearing garments made from big cat pelts was believed to give animal's strength and prowess to the wearer, although this led to heavy exploitation of these magnificent creatures.

HABITAT LOSS: A GROWING THREAT

As human populations expand, the natural habitats of big cats shrink. This is particularly acute for species like tigers and leopards, which require large territories for survival.

THE POACHING CRISIS

Illegal hunting for skins, bones, and other body parts poses a significant threat to big cats worldwide. Anti-poaching laws and increased border security are crucial to stop this illegal trade.

IMPACT OF ROADS AND INFRASTRUCTURE

Building roads and other structures can break up the homes of big cats, making it hard for them to reach places where they hunt and have babies.

CLIMATE CHANGE

Climate change is changing the habitats of many big cats, affecting their prey and forcing them into closer contact with humans. Animals like the snow leopard are especially at risk because warmer temperatures are melting their icy mountain homes.

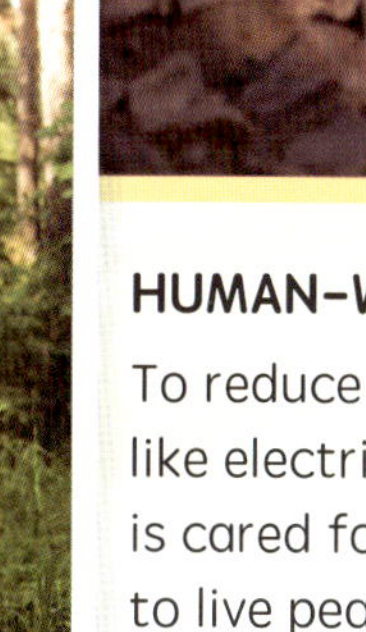

HUMAN–WILDLIFE CONFLICT RESOLUTION

To reduce conflicts, people use technology like electric fences, improve how livestock is cared for, and teach communities how to live peacefully with wildlife.

JAWS AND CLAWS: THE ANATOMY OF PREDATION

DESIGNED TO KILL

Big cats have long, sharp teeth called canines. These teeth help them catch and kill their prey. They usually bite the neck to break the spine or grab the throat to stop the prey from breathing.

Fun Fact

All big cats are great hunters, but cheetahs are special because their claws only partly hide. This helps them run super fast, like the cleats on a sports shoe, giving them better grip during their speedy chases.

THE ROLE OF CANINES

The canines of big cats are not only long and sharp but also exceptionally strong, capable of piercing hide and flesh with ease. These teeth are crucial during hunts, allowing cats to grip and hold struggling prey securely as they deliver the killing blow.

A ROUGH TONGUE

A big cat's tongue is covered with tiny, hook-like structures called papillae, which give it a rough texture. This adaptation helps them clean their fur and strip flesh from bones, ensuring they consume as much of their catch as possible. The rough tongue is also useful for grooming. It helps to remove loose fur and keep their coat clean.

PAWS OF POWER

The paws of big cats share many similarities with those of their smaller domestic cousins. Both have retractable claws that let them hide their claws when they are not needed. These can be extended to catch prey, climb, and defend. The structure of their paws allows for silent stalking, helping them to approach prey closely without making a sound.

CLAW RETRACTION MECHANISM

Big cats have special paws that let them hide their claws when they're not needed. This helps keep their claws sharp and ready to use when hunting or protecting themselves. Being able to hide their claws helps them catch and hold onto their prey better.

ECHOES OF THE PAST: EXTINCT BIG CATS

THE MIGHTY SABER-TOOTH: SMILODON FATALIS

Smilodon, often referred to as the saber-toothed tiger, roamed parts of North and South America until going extinct about 10,000 years ago. It had long, curved teeth and was a strong hunter. Instead of running fast, Smilodon would sneak up on its prey and use its powerful front legs to catch it.

Fun Fact

The saber-toothed tiger, Smilodon, had canines that could grow up to 7 inches long. They were so large and fragile that they had to be used very carefully to prevent them from breaking.

THE EUROPEAN CAVE LION: PANTHERA SPELAEA

The European cave lion was one of the biggest lions ever. It lived in Europe and Asia during the last Ice Age.These lions were shown in ancient cave paintings, suggesting they played a significant role in human mythology and culture before their extinction around 12,000 years ago.

THE AMERICAN LION: PANTHERA ATROX

The American lion was bigger than any lion today and lived in the Americas a long time ago during the Pleistocene period. The American lion is thought to have been one of the top predators of its time, preying on large herbivores that shared its North American range.

THE HOMOTHERIUM: SCIMITAR CAT

Homotherium, also known as the scimitar-toothed cat, had shorter, broader canine teeth than its saber-toothed cousins. It was likely more adapted to chasing prey in open environments. They were found across North and South America, Europe, Africa, and Asia, suggesting a highly adaptable nature.

THE JAVAN TIGER (PANTHERA TIGRIS SONDAICA)

The Javan tiger was native to Indonesia's Java Island. Similar in fate to the Bali tiger, it became extinct in the 1970s due to intense habitat pressure and poaching.

BEAUTY THAT PUTS LIVES AT RISK

WATER-LOVING CATS

Jaguars are unique among big cats because they love water. They often live near rivers, lakes, and wetlands. These strong swimmers enjoy bathing and even hunt for food in the water. Their love for water helps them catch prey like fish and caimans.

THE COVETED COAT

Jaguars have beautiful fur with unique spots, making their coats very special. In the 1960s, many people wanted jaguar fur for clothing, leading to a large number of jaguars being hunted. Now, it is illegal to hunt jaguars for their fur.

Fun Fact

In the 1960s, around 15,000 jaguars were killed each year for their beautiful fur.

SPOTTING THE DIFFERENCE

At first glance, jaguars and leopards look similar because of their spotted coats. However, key differences exist: jaguars possess larger, rounder heads and shorter tails, whereas leopards have smaller heads and longer tails.

TREE CLIMBERS TURNED GROUND HUNTERS

Young jaguars are playful and often climb trees to chase birds and small animals. As they grow bigger and heavier, climbing becomes harder. So, adult jaguars prefer to stay on the ground or swim in water to find food. They are powerful hunters, with the ability to take down larger prey like deer.

FURRY RELATIVES OF THE BIG CATS

A WORLD FULL OF WILD CATS

There are many kinds of wild cats living all over the world. Scientists have found about 40 different types, some big like lions and tigers, and some small like the ocelot and serval. Each wild cat has its own special home and way of living.

Fun Fact

The caracal is a wild cat that lives in dry, scrubby areas. This is why it's sometimes called the 'desert lynx.'

SERVAL: THE DAYTIME HUNTER

The serval is a special wild cat that likes to hunt when the sun is up. Most other cats prefer hunting at night or during dawn and dusk. Servals live in the grassy areas of Africa. They have long legs and big ears, which help them find and catch their food. Servals live in the African Savannah and look very similar to cheetahs.

THE SOLITARY OCELOT

The ocelot is a beautiful wild cat with a spotted coat. They live in the forests, grasslands, and swamps of South America. They usually live alone or sometimes in pairs. They are not picky eaters. Ocelots will eat almost anything they can catch, including small mammals, birds, and reptiles.

THE LYNX'S MAGICAL COAT

The lynx is a wild cat that can change its fur to match the seasons. In winter, its coat becomes thick and light-coloured to keep warm and blend in with the snow. In summer, the fur is shorter and darker. This amazing ability helps the lynx survive in the cold forests of Northern Europe and Asia.

Titles in this Series

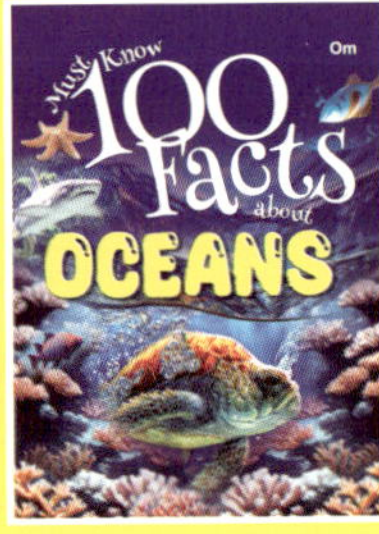

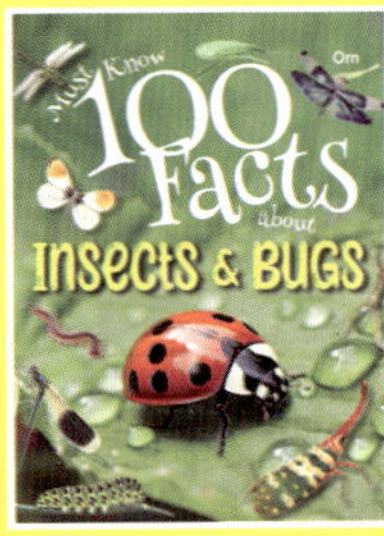

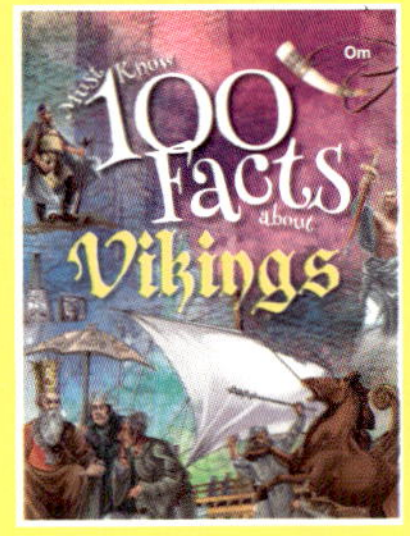

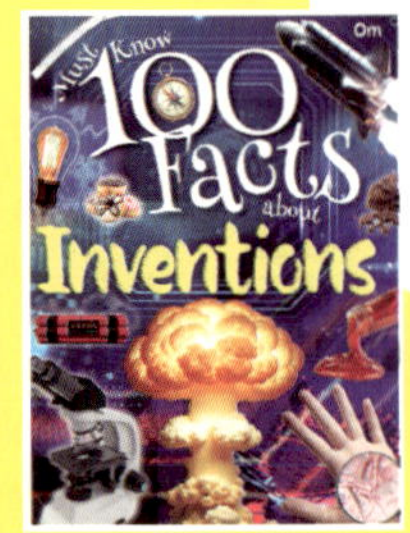

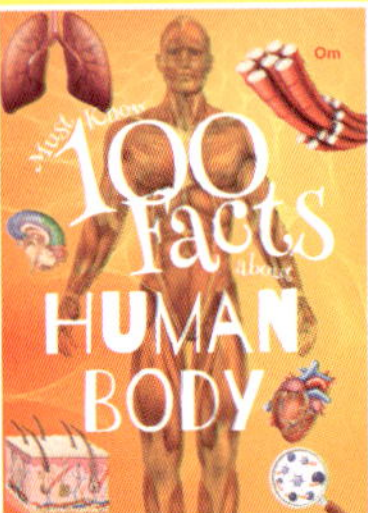

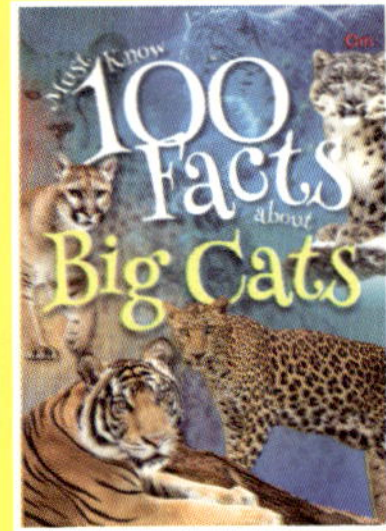

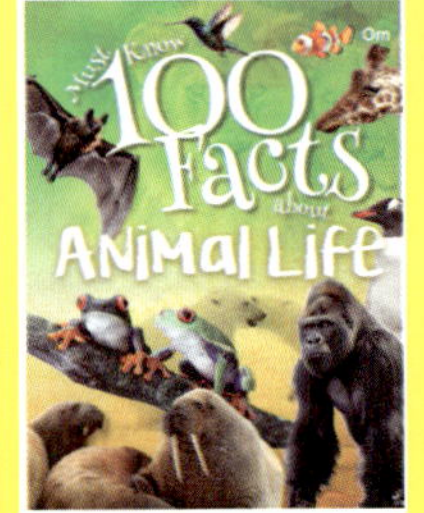

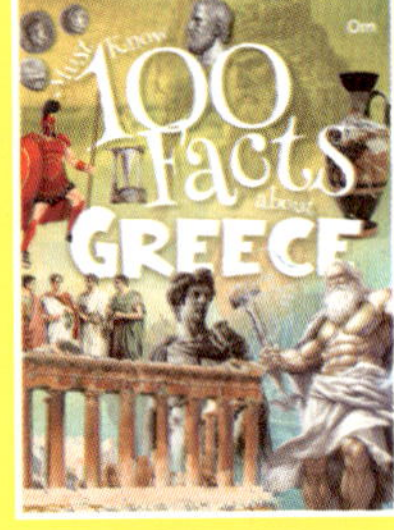

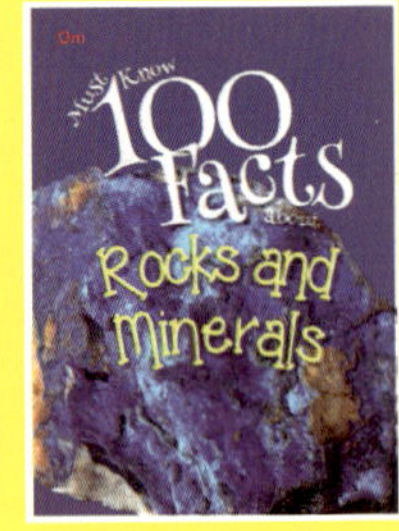